RELENTLESS FAVOR

DR. TRAVIS JENNINGS

Copyright © 2022 by Dr. Travis C. Jennings

ISBN: 9798422047796
Library of Congress Number: recorded in library database

All rights reserved by Apostle Jennings. No part of this publication may be reproduced, stored in or introduced into a retrieval system, or transmitted, in any form, or by any means (electronic, mechanical, photocopying, recording, or otherwise), without the prior written permission of both the copyright owner and the above publisher of this book.

Cover Design: Creative Freedom
Interior Layout Design: Write On Promotions

Dedication:

To all of the influential hands that have molded and shaped my ministry and mantle as it relates to faith that produces favor. Apostle John Eckhardt and Apostle I.V. Hilliard would be men that have shaped the quality of my life, if I were to name a few.

Introduction:

August 2nd, 2020

God spoke to me and said, "Travis, I need you to do a systematic teaching. I want you to declare this word in *this* season. Most people will minister in their current season. However, if you minister in your current season, you will never come out of it." God always gives you a word that will take you out of your current situation and bring you to your conclusion. The Lord took me to **Psalm 102:13**, which states,

"Thou shalt arise and have mercy upon Zion; for the set time to favor her, yea the set time is come."

The objective for this message is to inspire a revelation that will cause the believer to walk by faith, even in the season of famine. Believe in God for fantastic Favor. Do me a favor and say, *God is about to give me a revelation.* Remember, you can only go as far as your revelation. Whenever you get a revelation, faith will follow. Whatever you hear, you will start to believe. That is why we cannot preach in the current season; we must preach what is coming next. If we keep preaching our current pain, we will continue in that pain.

We must prophetically look past this moment and see the glory that is coming! **"For I reckoned that the suffering of this present time is not worth comparing the glory that will come afterwards"** (Romans 8:18).

There is a glory coming!

Relentless Favor

Chapter 1:

I GOT IT AND I KNOW IT: FAVOR!

I want to talk about one word – **Favor**. When we think about the word, "favor," we are more familiar with the idea of preferential treatment shown to someone. Favor is when someone shows good will towards you when someone accepts you. Favor is when someone gives you pleasure. Favor is when someone approves you over someone else. The Bible

Dr. Travis C. Jennings says, **"Many are called but few are chosen."**

God spoke to me and said, "That's what's getting ready to come upon you in another degree." I am not saying that you have never had favor, but God told me to tell you that the favor He is getting ready to hit your life with will upgrade what you already have. Do me a favor and say, *Upgrade! Upgrade! Upgrade!*

Let's break this down a little further. When you were in the 1st grade, that was called Favor, when you went to 2nd grade, that was called favor. When you went to the 3rd, 4th, and 5th grade, that was called favor. When you were in elementary that was called favor; but when you got to middle school that was a whole other favor. When you were in high school, that was a whole other favor. When you got to college that was again a whole other favor.

So, the Favor of God goes from one level to another level. That is why the KJV Bible speaks in Romans 1:17, "God is revealed from faith to faith." This means that the favor you start with will not be the favor you end with. I do not know who God sent this message for, but God told me to tell about 1,000 people reading this that He is getting ready to upgrade your favor! This favor is when God begins to ACCEPT, APPROVE, and give you PLEASURE. It is

Dr. Travis C. Jennings

almost a bias that God picks you over someone else. I know you only have an elementary education or a high school diploma, but God is getting ready to give you a career that only people with a four-year degree qualify for – God is about to flip the script. God is getting ready to give you a seven-figure salary. She went to school for 18 years and she is only making $50,000. You just barely got your GED, and you are making $1.5 million! You want to know why? Favor ain't fair.

God picks you over the other person; God favors you over the other person. God gives you something over the other person. Brothers and sisters, our working

Relentless Favor

definition of favor is when God raises up someone somewhere to use their power, influence, and ability to assist you. God is about to open some major doors for you. He says, "This time, you will not have to open the door. I'm going to use someone to open the door for you. I am talking about major doors, a door where you do not have the ability to open. I'm getting ready to give you a plug in every industry: Art, Entertainment, Media, Education, Family, Government, Business, and The Church. I am getting ready to raise up somebody who has greater expertise than you. They are getting ready to connect with you, and when they connect with you, the only thing they are going to tell you is – *follow my lead.*"

God gave me this revelation for you that will cause you to walk by faith, even in a season of famine. Believe in God for fantastic favor.

There are (3) key places where the Favor of God shows up:

1. Famine
2. Failure
3. Fracture

Relentless Favor

Let's take a look at **Genesis 26:12 KJV:**

Then Isaac sowed in that land, and received in the same year a hundredfold: and the Lord blessed him.

The Bible tells us that Isaac sowed in the land during a time when Israel was in a famine. Even in famine, favor showed up! I don't know who needs this word, but God told me to tell you that Favor will show up! You might be currently in a famine, but God says, "Sow your seed and wait for favor." Now, do me a favor and say, *Favor shows up in famine.*

Favor not only shows up in famine, but Favor shows up in failure. Let's take a look at **Luke 5:5 KJV:**

And Simon answering said unto him, "Master, we have toiled all the night, and have taken nothing: nevertheless at thy word I will let down the net."

The Bible tells us that Simon Peter was fishing all night, and he did not catch anything. In his current season, he is a failure, but the Word of the Lord came to him still. Simon obeyed God, went further, and launched out into the deep. He caught so many fish that other boats had to come and assist him. This is an example of how favor shows up, even in famine and failure.

Relentless Favor

My brothers and sisters, favor will also show up in a fracture as revealed in **Acts 3:7 KJV:**

And he took him by the right hand and lifted him up: and immediately his feet and ankle bones received strength.

Now the Bible tells us that this brother was laid outside of the beautiful gate because he had a fracture in his left ankle. Now, regardless of where you are, favor is about to find YOU! In Acts 3, the Bible tells us that Peter and John were going to the temple to pray. Peter said, "Silver and Gold, but such what I have I give unto thee." Peter took John by the left hand and John took Peter by the right.

Immediately, his ankle bones received strength. Favor showed up!

And I've come to prophesy that you might be in the pain of your life; you might be in the perplexity of your life; but God is ready to locate you and hit your life with favor!

Famine can't stop it! Failure can't stop it! Fracture can't stop it! Can I tell you something? Favor is getting ready to show up! However, favor has an enemy. You might be wondering, what goes against favor?

1. Doubt
2. Disobedience
3. The Devil

Relentless Favor

Doubt binds faith, and when doubt is present, deliverance cannot come. **Doubt hinders Favor**. Let's take a look at **Matthew 13:57-58:**

And they were offended in him. But Jesus said unto them, A prophet is not without honour, save in his own country, and in his own house. And he did not many mighty works there because of their unbelief.

What does this mean?

Favor can't show up when there is doubt. Doubt is an invisible, satanic poison that will seep into the veins of faith. It's when you can believe in what God can do for everybody else, but you can't believe in God for yourself. You'll believe in God for your mother, for your father, and you'll even believe in God for your sister. Many of you will believe in God for your brother in the church, for your sister in the choir, but you don't believe that God is able to do exceedingly, abundantly, above and beyond all that YOU could ever ask or think of. I came to prophesy that *doubt is an enemy of faith.*

And you'll say to yourself, "Can God – Will God? I have been sick for so long. Will I ever be healed? I have been stuck in this rented apartment; will I ever have my own? Or is this my plot in life?" Doubt will make you accept what you should be casting down. Doubt will cause you to acquiesce with something that was not designed for you. Doubt is an enemy of Favor.

Next, brothers and sisters, we must learn that **Disobedience is an enemy of Favor**. Let's take a look at **Jeremiah 5:24:**

Neither say they in their heart, Let us now fear the LORD our God, that giveth rain, both the former and the latter, in his season: he reserveth unto us the appointed weeks of the harvest.

God shared with Judah, "I want to give you something. I want to drop something down in your spirit, but I can't do it because every time I give you instructions, you always disobey me. Every time I give you a command, you always disobey me. Every time I send you a prophet to lead you in the path of righteousness, you always buck against it." I need someone to say they will destroy the enemy, disobedience!

I do not care how much you shout or dance or speak in tongues. If doubt is there, favor is absent. If disobedience is there, favor is absent! Everybody wants favor, but no one wants to live right. Just because you get a check doesn't mean you're getting favor. If your lifestyle does not please God, you will not receive favor. Whatever you are in is a satanic system to keep you locked down. The devil will bless you only to bind you! The blessings of the Lord don't have strings attached to them. "The blessings of the Lord maketh rich and added no sorrow" (Proverbs 10:22 KJV).

Every time God gives you instruction, every time He wakes you up in the morning to pray, you do everything *but* pray. Jeremiah says, "It is present, but it's not appointed. It is there but it's not going to touch down until you remove the disobedience." I want to minister to those who have been running from God. God has been giving you direction, but you have been running from him. Oh, brothers and sisters, you have to remove the doubt, you have to remove the disobedience, but thirdly, you have to remove the Devil. **The Devil hinders Favor**. The Devil is at work when you are being influenced by satanic and demonic forces.

God told me to tell you these words: Favor only comes when obedience, opportunity, and the outrageous manifest. Regardless of famine, regardless of failure, and even regardless of a fracture, God is getting ready to hit your life with Favor!

Favor is attracted to Obedience. Here in **2 Kings 2:2-4**, the Bible reads:

And Elijah said unto Elisha, Tarry here, I pray thee; for the L<small>ORD</small> *hath sent me* to Bethel. And Elisha said unto him, As the LORD liveth, and as thy soul liveth, I will not leave thee. So, they went down to Bethel.

And the sons of the prophets that were at Bethel came forth to Elisha, and said unto him, Knowest thou that the LORD will take away thy master from thy head today? And he said, Yea, I know it; hold ye your peace.

And Elijah said unto him, Elisha, tarry here, I pray thee; for the LORD hath sent me to Jericho. And he said, As the LORD liveth, and as thy soul liveth, I will not leave thee. So they came to Jericho.

Dr. Travis C. Jennings

If God is getting ready to hit your house, then the first thing you need to do is obey Him.

God is ready for you to see Him in a whole new way. He's getting ready to give you beauty for ashes and the oil of joy for mourning. He's getting ready to promote those who have been in the basement of life. He's getting ready to elevate those who have been pinching pennies. He's going to help those who have been fasting and praying, those who have been obeying God! Be not weary in well doing for you are in your due season! God is attracted to the believer who walks in obedience. God is attracted to you! God says that He is getting ready to hit your life with favor!

1. **Favor is attracted to Opportunity** – The Lord says that He is getting ready to open a door for you. For those who have obeyed, He's giving you an opportunity now. Opportunity is preparation, and preparation is getting ready to meet opportunity.

I want to talk to somebody. This message is for those who have been patiently praying, patiently prophesying, patiently praising. You have been asking God, "When are you going to do what you promised? God, when are you going to beat back the adversary? When are you going to save my son? Lord, when will you deliver my daughter? When will you give me a breakthrough? The prophet prophesized it and now, I am waiting on my turn to come around. I am waiting on strong deliverance; I am waiting on the tables to turn in my favor."

2. **Favor is attracted to the Outrageous** – This is for those who exemplify bold steps of faith. I want to talk to entrepreneurs who are stepping out on faith. You do not have a dime to your name, but you are believing in God to give you more on your way than when you started! The Lord says He's getting ready to give you

Relentless Favor

that for which you have been praying! Hallelujah!!

Dr. Travis C. Jennings

Chapter 2:

Thinking Rich

Did you know the brain is made up of two sides: the right side and the left side? Each side functions differently from the other. The right side is known to give us our art. It brings forth our creativity, our intuitiveness, and our connection to music. The right side of our brain is the creative side of our brain, the prophetic side, the discerning side of our brain. The right side of our brain even controls our left hand. However, the left side is analytical. This side deals with language, science, and math. The left side of our brain gives us our ability to use numbers and learn how to read and write. The left side of our brain controls our right hand. The left side of our brain is professional.

In this chapter, I want to talk to the left side of your brain. I want to talk to the professional side of your brain because you are going to get a left side victory! The left side of your brain is getting ready to be activated, and you are getting ready to walk into your prophetic destiny!

Relentless Favor

The Bible says in Proverbs 23:7, *"For as a man thinketh in his heart so is he."* So, whatever you think, you will become. Your thinking and your tongue work together. Say this with me aloud, *God is going to get ahold of my tongue!*

Did you know that on the Day of Pentecost, the Holy Ghost didn't manifest in their feet? No, the Holy Ghost did not manifest in their hands. The Holy Ghost didn't even manifest in their bellies. Where did the Holy Ghost manifest you might ask? The Holy Ghost manifested in their tongues. The Bible tells us in Acts 2:3, "And there appeared unto them cloven tongues like as of fire." God told me to tell you that if He can get ahold of your tongue, He can get ahold of your life. If you can change your tongue, you can change your trajectory. If you can change your tongue, you can change your life. You're getting ready to walk into another level of favor.

God is going to get the way you think together. God wants us to succeed and have an increase, and this starts with having an increased mind. He wants us to carry out the plan He has for our lives. We must work to replace the flawed mentality imposed on us by the world and cultivate the kingdom mentality that Jesus died and arose to give us. This kingdom mentality is the message God has given us concerning increase. We can see these messages laced throughout the scripture. In John 10:10, "The thief comes only to steal and kill and destroy; I (Jesus) have come so that they (we) may have life and have it in abundance."

Let's take a look at **Luke 6:38 (KJV):**

Give, and it shall be given unto you; good measure, pressed down, and shaken together, and running over, shall men give into your bosom. For with the same measure that ye mete withal it shall be measured to you again.

I've been studying the Bible for over 30 years. When I was studying about the above scripture, a revelation hit me in prayer. The Bible says, "shall men." I heard God say, "Travis, I'm getting ready to make you The Man!"

I want to prophesize that God is getting ready to raise you up to give into someone's bosom. God is about to turn you into a financier. God is about to turn you into a spiritual bank. So, when your brothers and sisters need loans, facilities, or automobiles, they don't have to go to Bank of America. They can just call you and you will finance it. God is getting ready to make you The Man!

Now, let us continue to open the eyes of our understanding through the Word of God. In Proverbs 10:22, it says, "The blessing of the LORD, it maketh rich, and he addeth no sorrow with it."

In the blessing of the Lord make**th** me rich, the "—**th**" added onto the word "rich" means God will continually make me rich. I've come to share with you that the days of 'one check only' are over, and the days of scattered showers are over too. A scattered shower is when God blesses you in a particular area, but nothing happens in any other area of your life. Another way you would see a scattered shower is when God gives you a download in your finances, but God is not giving you a download in your ministry. Can I share something with you? From this day forward, every facet of your life is going to experience the downpour of favor. In order to receive this, we must get our thoughts together.

Psalm 115:12-14:

The Lord hath been mindful of us: he will bless us; he will bless the house of Israel; he will bless the house of Aaron. He will bless them that fear the Lord, both small and great. The Lord shall increase you more and more, you and your children.

Not only does God want you to be favored, not only does God want you to be rich, but God is saying from the above scripture that He wants your children to be rich! God is saying to you, "I'm getting ready to put something on you. I'm getting ready to mantel you that not only you will walk into riches, but that your children will walk in riches, your children's children will walk in riches!" We see over and over in the word of God, that God wants to abundantly supply. Now listen, although increase is promised to the believer, it is not automatic. If the blessings were automatic, everybody would have them. However, God needs your permission and your participation. We must now walk in an intentional faith and a renewed mind.

Romans 12:1:

I beseech you therefore, brethren, by the mercies of God, that ye present your bodies a living sacrifice, holy, acceptable unto God, which is your reasonable service.

Do me a favor and say, *I need God to deliver my mind.* The way you think causes your life to stink. Stinking thinking is something we're all guilty of. Unknowingly, we have all been environmentally coded. You are the sum total of how you were raised, what you were taught, and your background.

For example, I was raised in an urban community (the hood). I was raised in a community where the word 'rich' denoted illegal activity. Since I wasn't raised with a silver spoon in my mouth, the only people in my community who were rich were drug dealers and pimps. So, for me, the word "rich" is connected to immoral or illegal gain. The word "rich" was not a positive word for me.

When I received salvation in the sanctified church, the word "rich" had a new meaning. In the sanctified church, the word "rich" denoted people who didn't walk in the will of God or people who hustled and loved money. Before salvation, I had a bad definition of the word. Then, after salvation, I had a bad definition of the word rich. In the sanctified church they told me, "God doesn't want you to be rich; He just wants to save you." But we can see from the Word that this is far from the truth. If that were the case, the above scripture would not stand true. I had to remove stinking thinking. The word "rich" can be very intimidating; however, it doesn't necessarily mean multi-millionaire only. The word "rich" in scripture means to have resource for yourself, to help others, and have plenty left over.

I want to prophesy that God is getting ready to make you so rich that you will help yourself, help others, and have plenty left over! You won't need the aid of anyone else. You will be able to take care of yourself, your family, your loved ones, and have plenty left over. I prophesy that your leftovers will be greater than what you give out! We must remove the old stinking thinking and what we think of rich and now understand that the new meaning of rich means to be able to take care of yourself, others and have plenty left over.

God is blessing someone with promotion, NOW!

God is giving somebody a new house, NOW!

God is giving somebody a new car, NOW!

Matter of fact, God is not only going to give you a house, but He is also going to give you houses that you haven't built and vineyards that you haven't planted.

Dr. Travis C. Jennings

If you're still asking, "When is he going to do it?" The answer is: NOW! God is about to open some doors NOW! The money is coming NOW! The healing is coming NOW! The breakthrough is coming NOW! God is saying, "I'm not going to bless you 'by and by.' I'm not going to bless you in the New Jerusalem." Jesus is saying, "I'm going to give you the 100-fold NOW!" You've been waiting for things to happen; you've been waiting for things to move; but God says, "It is happening NOW! However, you must remember this, it will be connected to persecution."

Prosperity is always connected persecution. The 100-fold blessings will come with persecution. The 100-fold breeds persecution; it breeds slander; it breeds gossip. The financial increase mentality develops a tolerance of persecution. Remember this, persecution will only affect you to the degree that you need approval from the one's persecuting you.

Everyone wants the 100-fold, but no one wants the 100-fold persecution. Everyone is not going to be happy with your riches. Go ahead and drink the cup and know that everyone who walks with you to the step, may not be able to climb the step with you. Those that prayed for you in your time of struggle, may not be there with you in your time of success. They'll say things like, "You're changing." You'll have to tell them, "Yes I am changing – I'm transforming into my truest self."

Transform into the man of God. Transform into the woman of God. You are not that broke, dysfunctional puppy that you used to be. Many people love to clean up your mess. But when God matures you and you're not making messes any longer, their manipulation is no longer needed. God is getting ready to put the 100-fold on you, and you're not going to need them any longer. You must be all right with letting certain people go.

I've said this before, and I will say it again; you don't need approval from the one persecuting you. I need you to begin to see money as a resource and a tool not a status or judgement. We can't look at riches as a standard of judgement. Luke 12:15 says, "And he said unto them, Take heed, and beware of covetousness: for a man's life consisteth not in the abundance of the things which he possesseth."

Many people use money as a judgement to determine self-worth, maturity, etc. Others see money as a stronghold imposed on one's will over the other. Now, this is one of the greatest deceptions of riches and often causes pride and arrogance. Others see money as a stool, which can be misplaced security confidence in money. This perception can be very destructive and can come from idolatry.

We see this example in the story in the above scripture. Many people will see money as saying, "I've made it," then judge themselves and their self-worth as important. No, your self-worth has nothing to do with money. Your value has nothing to do with money. In the world, they judge you by your clothes, cash, cribs, cars, and even your credit. They've said that according to these things, you've made it, but that is not so here in the kingdom. We do not worship money. Riches are not to be trusted; they are a tool. We must see money as a tool, an agent for purposeful and constructive exchange to accomplish worth-while goals and objectives.

The Bible says that money is a servant, that money answers all things. We think that money is evil. No, the **love** of money is evil. Money is a servant and money answers all thing. Somebody say, *I have a big question!* The Bible says money is not to be trusted, but that money is a tool. So how do you spell tool? T-O-O-L— those that love to garden for all my non-city people. Every time you have to garden or work with soil that you have planted seed in, you're going to have to use certain tools to bring about the manifestation and cultivation of that garden. You want that garden to give you maximum results.

Well, Holy Ghost told me to tell you that, God has given you a garden (metron/ministry) and you've been asking God, "How can I take my garden to the next level?" God is saying that you need a tool to cultivate what He has put inside of you and that tool is called Riches." This tool is getting ready to take your life to the next level. God is about to give you a divine tool and that tool is about to cultivate into a manifestation.

MONEY IS A TOOL! Money is a measure that gives you the power to manifest the desire of your heart. **1 Tim**

6:17 says, "Charge them that are rich in this world, that they be not high-minded, nor trust in uncertain riches, but in the living God, who giveth us richly all things to enjoy." We have to change this way of thinking – the saints shouldn't go to Paris; the saints shouldn't wear designer clothing; the saints shouldn't enjoy life. But you're still living on section 8. People think that all we're supposed to do is come to church, dance, and speak in tongues.

I'm not coming against section 8 because I came from that, but I got a revelation. I was on government assistance, but I got a revelation. We have to be careful of the religious witches because they'll look at your riches and prosperity and say, "You shouldn't be swimming and owning yachts and boats... that's just flesh." But the Bible tells us that God gives us richly ALL things to enjoy.

Now remember, your enjoyment may not be indicative to my enjoyment. You may just enjoy a Toyota, and I might enjoy a Tesla. You might enjoy a bike; I might enjoy a Bentley. You might enjoy a Mazda; I might enjoy a Maserati. You might enjoy a three-bedroom flat house; I might enjoy a 30-bedroom house. Why? Because I want to entreat the saints from out of town. I want to ensure that when people come in, they don't have to go to the Ritz Carlton or Four

Relentless Favor

Seasons; they can just come to the Jennings Estate. I love taking care of people. I love hosting people. I love entreating people. I am a people's person.

Do me favor and say, *God wants me rich, so that I can take care of me, others, and have plenty left over!* I want to prophesy that God is getting ready to touch your reserves, and give you millions in your reserves. You got a revelation that riches are not to be trusted, but riches are a tool. God says that the next time He drops something in your heart; you're not going to have to go to the bank for a loan. You'll be able to finance it yourself!

So, Scripture talks about that money is also a fuel. We must view it as a seed placed in the proper soil that really brings forth a harvest and when we see it as a seed, we understand what Genesis 8:22 says, **"As the earth remains there will be seed time and harvest."** When you look at money as something that you are losing because you trust in it. It's going to hinder you from sowing it. Are you emotionally attached to the money? I need you right now to break the emotional attachment to money. When you are emotionally attached to money, you trust in it. This why people don't tithe, and therefore people don't sow seed, because they trust in the money. The money is not your source, it is a resource.

When I sow my tithe and give my offering, if I look at it like I'm losing, I am emotionally attached to it.

Can I be transparent? God delivered me when I was studying this. Now I've been delivered from poverty, I walk in favor. But when I go to the bank, I still get my bank balance. I want you hear the spirit in which I'm coming from. The Lord gave me this when I trusted in riches. You are always emotionally attached to the bank balance because your bank balance normally creates your mood. If you are emotionally attached to the bank balance, you could be trusting in riches. When you're not trusting in riches, the bank balances are going to fluctuate. You understand that I just sowed, and I'm now ready for harvest.

When I've sown, I know that the number or value can't stay the same because what's coming will be greater than what went out. Now, I stand in expectation of the harvest that is on the way. So, I am not emotionally attached to the seed I've sown. The seed I've sown in good ground is coming back with a harvest of 30, 60, or 100-fold. We're living in a time of **Amos 9: 13**, where as fast as you sow it, you are going to reap it! I don't go home saying to myself, "What did you do that for?"

The Favor of God is coming upon you, and the only thing you need to do is

Relentless Favor

GIVE! You have five levels coming on you because you have your thinking together! I want to talk to somebody. God told me to tell you:

You will never ever be scared when the first of the month comes!

You are not going to worry!

You'll be able to pay your bills a month in advanced!

You'll be able to pay your mortgage a month in advanced – until there is no mortgage!

I prophesy you will be debt free, and you will not have a mortgage!

Dr. Travis C. Jennings

You've been asking God, "What about all this?" But God is saying trust Me and get your thinking together!

Chapter 3:

You Can't Fight Favor

In going back to our original text of Psalm 102, "Thou shalt arise and have mercy upon Zion; for the time to favour her, yea, the set time, is come." In this season, God has spoken to me and said, "Travis, regardless of whether or not the world is in famine, the saints are in favor." Regardless of whether or not the world is in a pandemic, the kingdom is in the promises of God. The Bible says you have not because you ask not. The Bible also says that life and death are in the power of your tongue. Then the Bible goes on to say the tongue is the pen of the ready writer.

In building this teaching of favor, I want to build on the working definition, looking at favor from a holistic view. Favor doesn't only manifest prosperity, but it also protects you. When looking at favor, many people only think about money, or advanced, or talking about an open door or opportunity. Favor, however, is also multifaceted, just like grace. Favor is grace, and grace is favor. Many people look at favor in a one-sided-way. They think Favor only gives you prosperity. We see in the Scripture below that Favor also brings protection, like mentioned in Psalm 5:11-12:

But let all those that put their trust in thee rejoice: let them ever shout for joy, because thou defendest them: let them also that love thy name be joyful in thee. For thou, LORD, wilt bless the righteous; with favour wilt thou compass him as with a shield.

And Psalm 41:11

By this I know that thou favourest me, because mine enemy doth not triumph over me.

Dr. Travis C. Jennings

It's like when your car almost ran off of the road, and you were two inches away from going over the bank; that was favor. When the doctor gave you a bad diagnosis and God healed your body, that was favor. When the enemy came in like a flood in your house – your house was on fire and you ran out, but there was no smoke damage in your body; that was favor. When doctor found a lump in your breast – you went through 36 rounds of chemo and 45 treatments of radiation. Now, you've been cancer free for 18 years, that's favor. The Favor of God is more than just money. The Favor of God is more than a promotion. The Favor of God must be looked at holistically. The Favor of God not only brings prosperity, but the Favor of God brings protection.

In Chicago, New York, and even here, on the east side of Atlanta, bullets are flying everywhere, and you are just trying to get some Dairy Queen. The bullet didn't even touch you; that was favor. There was a pile up on the highway, an 18-car pileup. Cars smashing into one another, and you were the 19th car; that was the Favor of God. Tell somebody right now, "I have the Favor of God on my life."

The Favor of God will show up in famine, failure, and in a fracture. Cherish even now that God is willing to bless the righteous, but also protect them with the weapon of favor. Favor is a weapon. You see the weapon of favor when the enemy tells you that you are not going to come out of the divorce. Again, when the enemy comes in and brings warfare in your finances; favor is a weapon. When the enemy comes in and brings warfare in your body; favor is a weapon. When the enemy comes in and brings warfare in your faith; favor is your weapon. Somebody say, FAVOR IS A WEAPON.

That's why David said, "The Lord is my light and my salvation, of whom shall I fear, the Lord is the strength of my life of whom shall I be afraid, when my enemy came upon me to eat up my flesh, they stumbled and fell." You see, David understands that God is not just a God of prosperity, but a God of protection! There is no disease, infirmity, or blood condition that can stand against the weapon of favor. The devil has been trying to come against your respiratory system, your circulatory system, your reproductive system, your skeletal system, and nervous system. Tell yourself that you have to fight with the weapon of favor.

The Favor of God is upon man, and he will be secured and protected from all opposition. Opposition is only an indicator that breakthrough is around the corner. We can see this kind of favor operating in the life of Daniel. Daniel and all of Israel were prisoners in Babylon; even though he had favor with all of the officials. Daniel 1:9 lets us know, "Now God had brought Daniel into favour and tender love with the prince of the eunuchs."

We see how God favored Daniel, even in a strange land. We can't fight favor. You can tell somebody, "You can put my bed in hell and favor will find me there. You can lie, gossip, slander, and backstab against me but the Favor of God is on me." Can I speak to someone right here? Have people been talking about you? Trying to dig a ditch for you? Well, I have a word from the Lord for you, "They can't fight favor." In other accounts from the text, we know that Daniel had so much favor in the land that he was elevated to a prestigious position in Babylon kingdom. Even though the circumstances were stacked against him, we know that Daniel became the Prime Minister over Babylon.

God told me to tell you that you will prosper, even in a pandemic. I came to tell you that favor is getting ready to show up because you can't fight favor.

Let's look at Esther 2:17: "And the king loved Esther above all the women, and she obtained grace and favour in his sight more than all the virgins; so that he set the royal crown upon her head and made her queen instead of Vashti." Now, you see here that Esther was selected among several other beautiful ladies that were all ready to be queen, but God chose Esther.

Let's go to another example in 1 Samuel 16:11: "And Samuel said unto Jesse, Are here all thy children? And he said, there remaineth yet the youngest, and behold, he keepeth the sheep. And Samuel said unto Jesse, send and fetch him: for we will not sit down till he come hither."

We see here that a man was chosen for a position for which he is not naturally qualified. The text shows us that David was the most unqualified person in his family, naturally. But God rejected everybody else and looked at him. His father forgot about him; his brother deserted him; but God favored him. I want to talk to somebody who has a bad resume. I want to talk to somebody who has a bad report. I want to talk to somebody that has a felony. I want to talk to somebody who didn't cross every t and dot every i. The Favor of God is getting ready to find you!

Let's look at Jabez; 1 Chronicles 4:9-10 says: "And Jabez was more honourable than his brethren: and his mother called his name Jabez, saying, 'Because I bare him with sorrow.' And Jabez called on the God of Israel, saying, 'Oh that thou wouldest bless me indeed, and enlarge my coast, and that thine hand might be with me, and that thou wouldest keep me from evil, that it may not grieve me!' And God granted him that which he requested."

Now, many can't dance about Jabez because many people don't understand Jabez. But when you read 1st Chronicle, the 4th chapter, it begins with the father, *and he begot*. When you get to verse 9 there is no genealogy, Jabez father isn't even mentioned. The first thing mentioned is, "And Jabez was more honorable than all of his brethren and his mother called his name Jabez because she bore in sorrow." Verse 10 goes on to record Jabez saying, "Oh God of all Israel, that though would bless me indeed and enlarge my coast, and that thou hand be upon me...and God granted him that wish he requested." Jabez father was never mentioned, but when the Favor of God is upon you, its greater than your father.

I want to talk to somebody whose father never blessed them, validated them, or took care of them. The Bible says in Psalm 27:10, "When my mother and father forsake me, then the Lord will take me up." I want to talk to somebody who was rejected and even neglected, but God told me to tell you, that His favor is getting ready to find you. Just like Jabez, He is getting ready to enlarge your territory! He is getting ready to place His hand upon you! Esther found favor even amongst the equal and the greater. David was the least likely, but favor was upon him. Jabez was a bastard. His father was not even mentioned, but the favor makes up the neglect.

God is getting ready to do what you didn't expect Him to do. You were expecting them to give you 10% but God is getting ready to give you the whole 100. You were expecting God to pay your light bill, but He is getting ready to set you up so good it's going to come out of your residual. You are not going to have to pay your bills because your accountant is about to pay your bill for you. God is about to give you so much money that you'll need a financial adviser. You will need someone to take care of all your dividends. God is about to give you so much favor that even the thing you never expected will happen.

When a man is guided to take a little effort, it leads to great achievement. Peter didn't catch anything, he was a failure, but the word of the Lord came to Peter and great success was his portion. Favor found Moses on the backside of the dessert. Favor found David when he was looking after the sheep. Favor found Paul on the road to Damascus. Another thing that favor does is it will single you out of the crowd. Say this, *God is about to single me out.* You're in an overly crowed room and God will single you out. There's a lot of people going for the position, but God will single you out! You're trying to go for a raise and God is about to single you out! Say it again, *God is about to single me out!* There are 35,000 people in the building, but God is about to single you out. There are 500 people in your department, but God is about to single you out! The field of your expertise is jammed packed. Everybody is doing what you're doing, but when the Favor of God is upon you, God will single you out.

You're the last to get hired, but you will be the first to get promoted. God will allow the manager to train and develop you, not knowing that they are training and developing their replacement. You see, God's alphabet is different from man's alphabet. Your alphabet might begin with A, B, C, D, E, F, G. God's alphabet is different because God will put a Z before an A, an M before a D, and a J before an L. Your record, your resume, and your riches are coming up before God!

God is shifting the tables in your life and your name is coming up before Him. When God brings your name before Him, He'll give you beauty for ashes, the oil of joy, and the garment of praise for the spirit of heaviness. The last shall be first, and the first shall be last. Many are called but few are chosen. God is about to place a Z before an A! It doesn't matter how many people are there, God's Favor just focused in on you. You won't understand it all the time. God will single you out just for a miracle.

Go with me to the story with the blind man in Mark 10:46-47:

And they came to Jericho: and as he went out of Jericho with his disciples and a great number of people, blind Bartimaeus, the son of Timaeus, sat by the highway side begging. And when he heard that it was Jesus of Nazareth, he began to cry out, and say, Jesus, thou Son of David, have mercy on me.

Relentless Favor

The Bible tells us that there were multitudes and anytime you read of a multitude it consists of 5,000 people. The Bible tells us that Jesus is walking with a minimum of 5,000 people and this blind man is crying out. Out of all the thousands of people around him, he singles out this blind man and this blind man gets the miracle. God told me to tell you that by the end of this month, He's giving miracles to those who will praise Him. He says, "I'm going to give to the one who will give me glory, the one who will give me praise, the one who will lift their hands. I'm giving miracles to them. I'm getting ready to beat back the hand of adversity."

Dr. Travis C. Jennings

Believers, eyes have not seen; ears have not heard! God is getting ready to single you out! You, who have never experienced love from your mother, or your father never claimed you, or you were the black sheep of the family. Prepare to be singled out. Those of you who had to pinch pennies; you who had to take care of yourself; you who had to pay your own way through college because no one ever believed that you were going to make it. No one ever believed that you were going to amount to anything. They looked at your father and mother when they looked at you, and they never gave you a fair opportunity. You might be the forgotten one but favor always finds the forgotten.

Relentless Favor

It looks like you've been overlooked. The enemy has convinced you that you have been forgotten. However, I'm glad that in Hebrew 6:10 says; "For God is not unrighteous to forget your work and labour of love, which ye have shewed toward his name, in that ye have ministered to the saints, and do minister." God told me to tell you, that He has seen your tears, and He has heard your cry, and is getting ready to reward those who have felt like they've been forgotten. You've been praying and nobody knows it. You've been serving but nobody sees it, for years you've been serving, and it seems like your miracle is being held up. God told me to tell you, that He doesn't sleep on the forgotten. I came to tell you that favor always finds the forgotten! You can't fight favor.; Favor in your **Medical**; Favor in your **Material**; and Favor in your **Marital**.

- **Medical**- If you are sick and considered incurable, you will find favor with God. You will suddenly discover that the incurable will begin to have a testimony. (**John 5:2-9**)

- **Material** - When you find Favor with God, suddenly, whatever you touch begins to prosper and people will begin to wonder how? (**Luke 5:1-7**)

Relentless Favor

- **Marital**- If you have been considered barren and God decides to favor you, suddenly those of you who have been laughing against you will begin to laugh with you. (**1 Samuel 5:1-6**)

Dr. Travis C. Jennings

Chapter 4:

Accessing Favor

Are you ready to go deeper? Well, let's get into it. We've talked about favor, and we know favor is more than just manifesting prosperity, and that favor also provides protection. We've looked at favor from a holistic point of view. Now, we're going to dig deeper and look at favor as a pathway. In this chapter, we're going to be learning about how to access the Favor of God. Did you know that you can have money in the bank? You can have millions and millions of dollars, but if you cannot access it; it is no good to you. I want to encourage that you have kingdom authority, and you *can* access the Favor of God on your life. Do me a favor and say, *I am tapping into my favor. I am accessing favor.*

I often like to watch the Discovery Channel. One night, while I was up at 2 a.m., this show came on the T.V. It was about people claiming freight and unclaimed treasure. People had received inheritances of millions of millions of dollars, but they could not access it because they didn't know. Sometimes, the riches of God belong to us, but we don't know how to access it by faith. When we can't access it, it ends up being no good to us. It's not that the Favor of God is not there, we have to learn how to access it by faith. All of the promises of God are received by faith. In this chapter, we will be dealing with the pathway of Faith.

> 1. Favor is the **Actions** of God to do for man, what man was unable to do for himself. (Ephesians 2:8-9)

When you see the word "grace," it is another word for favor. So, the Bible tells us that by grace we are saved through favor, not of yourself. This means that favor is the actions of God to do for man what man was not able to do for himself. The Lord spoke to me and said, "Favor is about to do for what you are not physically able to do for yourself." Do me a favor and say, *Favor is about to move in my life.*

1. Favor is the **Availability** of righteousness through the work of Jesus Christ (Roman 5:17).

We see that we have availability through righteousness because of what Jesus did. It was because of the favor that Jesus gave us that we are now righteous.

1. Favor is the **Ability** to function at a higher level

without formal training. (1 Corinthians 15:9-10)

When the Favor of God opens a door, it is beyond your educational level, your pedigree, or formal training.

For I am the least [worthy] of the apostles, and not fit to be called an apostle, because I [at one time] fiercely oppressed and violently persecuted the church of God. But by the [remarkable] grace of God I am what I am, and His grace toward me was not without effect. In fact, I worked harder than all of the apostles, though it was not I, but the grace of God [His unmerited favor and blessing which was] with me. (1 Corinthians 15:9-10)

What Paul is saying in the above scripture is that he is moving in the apostolic. He is moving into a higher position. Paul says, "I am the least." He is saying he should not be doing all of this but it's because of favor. When the Favor of God shows up, God opens doors for which you are not qualified. Look at David, he moved into kingship, and wasn't qualified for it because his father wasn't a king. Back in those days, in order to be a king, it had to come through the genealogy. Your father had to be the king because you would be the prince, and after he transitioned, then you would become king. David's father was a herdsman. Nevertheless, when the Favor of God shows up, it causes you to function at a higher level. I decree and declare right now for those that are reading this, you are about to function at a higher level. Favor doesn't come from the east or the west: favor comes from God.

Many people are looking at you and scratching their heads. They are wondering how you are flowing the way you are. How do you speak the way you do? How do you know the things you know? You must let them know that favor gives you the ability to function at a higher level. God is getting ready to bring you into rooms that your pedigree could not merit you. God is about to bring you before great men and when they look at you, they're going to ask, "My

God, where have you been?" God is about to shift your functionality.

1. Favor is the **Authority** given to you against spiritual adversaries to bind and loose!

Concerning this I pleaded with the Lord three times that it might leave me.

(2 Corinthians 12:8)

In the above Scripture, Paul prays to God to get this thing out of him. God is about to put favor on you that gives you the authority to bind and loose. The Bible says in Matthews 18:18, "Whatsoever [we] bind on earth will be bound in heaven, and

Relentless Favor

whatsoever [we] lose in heaven must be loosed on earth." You are waiting for God to bind and lose some things. God is saying, "I'm not binding nor am I losing." God has given you the authority through favor to bind and loose. Whatever you bind, He'll back you up! Likewise, whatever you lose, He'll back you up. God is waiting for his people to move in this type of favor. Operate in the Favor of God that gives you authority. The next time you open your mouth, demons will be bound, sicknesses will be removed, and tumors will be dissolved. You need to walk in your favor that God has given you.

Dr. Travis C. Jennings

1. Favor is the **Agent** in life for peace being sustained in a stressful situation. Favor is the agent in your life that brings peace even during a pandemic (Roman 5:1 AMP).

Therefore, since we have been justified [that is, acquitted of sin, declared blameless before God] by faith, [let us grasp the fact that] we have peace with God [and the joy of reconciliation with Him] through our Lord Jesus Christ (the Messiah, the Anointed).

(Roman 5:1 AMP)

Romans 5:1 lets us know that even when we are going through a stressful period, the Favor of God brings the peace.

Favor is an agent, and it brings peace: the peace that you need for your assignment, the peace that you need for your children. No, you're not going crazy; you have the peace of God. You're not going to lose your mind; you have the peace of God. You're not going to push the panic button; you have the peace of God. Favor is an agent that brings peace.

2. Favor is the **Advantage** we have for supernatural abundance in life (*2 Corinthian 9:8*).

Have you noticed that I've been loading you down with scripture? It is because your faith cannot rest in man; it must rest in the Word of God. Faith begins where the will of God is known. And when you see it in the Word of God, then you can begin to release your faith for that promise in the Word. When you see it in the Word, you understand Numbers 23:19: "God is not a man that he should lie, neither is he the son of man that he would repent. If he said it, he'll do it. If he spoke it, he shall bring it to pass and make it good."

God says He is getting ready to hit your life with so much Favor that you'll never be under the eight ball. God is getting ready to hit your life with so much favor that you won't have to rob Peter to pay Paul. God is getting ready to hit your life with so much favor that you're not going to be stressed out when the 1st of the month comes around. The Bible tells us that because of this favor, you have sufficiency in all things, and you will abound to every good work.

Favor will give you an advantage – everyone else is going under, but the Favor of God will make sure you are self-sufficient. Whatever your need or the situation is, or whatever season you're in, favor will meet you. The Word of God tells me that every season I'm in is a good season. Can I share something with you? You may have a bill that may come out of left field, but you will have the money to take care of it. Whatever the need is, whatever the circumstance maybe; favor gives you the advantage to always have it.

I prophesy that you will always have it, glory to God! He is taking you to the next level that you are not even going to need a bank to finance your dream. You are going to be able to finance your own dream. God is about to fill up every account. He's about to fill you with prosperity and take care of you in such a way that when He downloads the dream, you'll be able to furnish it.

Sometimes we can dance and shout, but we don't listen to the word of God. That's why many people are still broke. You have to get it in the Word. The Favor of God is about to hit your life so that you will require no aid! Just shout: "Self-sufficiency!" You wish to be self-sufficient, possessing enough to require no aid or support and furnish in abundance to every good work. That means everything God puts in your spirit to do, you will have the finances to walk it through. This is the kind of favor we must access. Say it with me, *I have Favor that gives me the advantage.*

People think that their jobs are their source, but no, Jehovah Jireh is your source! God gave you that job so that you can sow seed. But you don't live on that. We live on the overflow, and we must access the Favor of God. Now, let me just say this, when you begin to access this kind of favor two things will happen. People that you thought were your friends will no longer be your friends. Some people like for you to need them. Some people like for you to beg them. They are spiritual witches, and they like to manipulate you because they like to feel needed. However, you're about to get to a place called graduation. You're about to get to a place called promotion. You're about to get to a place in the realm of the spirit, that realm of the supernatural, where you won't need any aid or support. God is about to cause you to be self-sufficient!

Chapter 5:

Favor is About to Locate You

And David said, "Is there still anyone left of the house (family) of Saul to whom I may show kindness for Jonathan's sake?" There was a servant of the house of Saul whose name was Ziba, so they called him to David. And the king said to him, "Are you Ziba?" He said, "I am your servant." And the king said, "Is there no longer anyone left of the house (family) of

Saul to whom I may show the goodness and graciousness of God?" Ziba replied to the king, "There is still a son of Jonathan, [one] whose feet are crippled." So the king said to him, "Where is he?" And Ziba replied to the king, "He is in the house of Machir the son of Ammiel, in Lodebar." Then King David sent word and had him brought from the house of Machir the son of Ammiel, from Lodebar. Mephibosheth the son of Jonathan, the son of Saul, came to David and fell face down and lay himself down [in respect]. David said, "Mephibosheth." And he answered, "Here is your servant!" David said to him, "Do not be afraid, for I will certainly show you kindness for the sake of your father Jonathan, and will restore to you all the land of your grandfather Saul; and you shall always eat at my table." Again Mephibosheth lay himself face down and said, "What is your servant, that you would be concerned for a dead dog like me?"

(2 Samuel 9:1-8)

I heard from God about favor. He said, "Even though the world is in a pandemic, the kingdom is in the promise. Even though the world is in jeopardy, the kingdom is in glory. Even though the world is in pain, the kingdom is in prosperity." He told me to tell you these words, "I am able to do exceeding, abundantly, above and beyond all you can ask of think according to the power that works on the inside of them." As I began to share with God, God began to share with me. He said, "Travis, I need you to write these words, *Get ready for a divine locator.*" I began to do a study on electronic locators. Many companies use locators in different objects, or even pets, just in case things are stolen, lost, or misplaced. They are even used with repossessions. Locators are often located on the company's GPS system and that system has the specific position and location of that object. This makes it so nothing can really be stolen or lost because there is a locator on that object.

Relentless Favor

I remember years ago during one of our church encounters; after everyone was done dancing and shouting, I had a musician that went out to get in his automobile, and it was gone. He thought someone came and stole his car during the encounter. Come to find out, the musician didn't pay his car note and the bank tapped into the car's internal GPS locator and came to get their property back. Now, he thought that someone stole his car, but unbeknownst to him, before they gave him the keys, they connected the car to their GPS just in case he did not pay his bill.

As God brought this story to mind, He told me to tell His people that He is getting ready to divinely locate them. Regardless of a failure, famine, or fracture; He can locate you. No matter where you are, God can locate you! Favor is getting ready to locate you:

When Noah was building the ark, favor located him.

When Moses was standing at the Red Sea, favor located him.

Favor located Joshua right before he got to the Jericho wall.

Favor located the three Hebrew boys: Shadrach, Meshach, and Abednego, in the fiery furnace.

Relentless Favor

Favor located Elijah on Mount Carmel.

Favor located Jehoshaphat when he was surrounded by the enemy.

Favor located Daniel in the den of lions.

Favor located Esther in the king's palace.

Favor located Peter when he was toiling all night and caught nothing.

Favor located Paul and Silas when they were locked up in a Philippian prison.

Favor located the disciple's right there on the lake when they couldn't pay their taxes and God said open the mouth of the fish and there was a piece of gold.

I don't know who you are, but favor is getting ready to locate you!

In the above scripture we read about Mephibosheth and God finding him despite his current situation and circumstances. We learn that Mephibosheth comes from a disgraced family, a doomed family, and a destitute family. Finding the only remaining blood of Saul's family was not a simple matter, but David located a grandson by the name of Mephibosheth, the son of Jonathan.

We first learn of him in 2 Samuel 4 that Saul's son, Jonathan, had a son whose feet were crippled. He was crippled, living in obscurity and poverty in a remote and barren corner of the kingdom.

Jonathan, Saul's son, had a son whose feet were crippled. He was five years old when the news [of the deaths] of Saul and Jonathan came from Jezreel. And the boy's nurse picked him up and fled; but it happened that while she was hurrying to flee, he fell and became lame. His name was Mephibosheth.

(2 Samuel 4:4 Jonathan)

I want to talk to someone who is frustrated. You have power and the ability, but nothing has been working out for you. You've been seeding and serving; you've been singing and shouting, but nothing has been happening for you. God told me tell you, "Don't worry, I've got somebody looking for you!"

The scripture above reveals (4) things:

David **Sought** him.

David **Sent** for him.

David **Spoke** to him.

David **Spared** him.

The Bible says in verses 1-4 that when David found out that Johnathan had a son, he began the process of finding him. David began to seek for Mephibosheth. When discovered where he was, he began

Relentless Favor

the process of bringing Mephibosheth to him. God told me to tell you, that there is process that has already been in place, and God is getting ready to bring you to the people of influence. God says, "Rise and shine for the light has come and the glory of the Lord has risen upon you." Somebody has you on their mind and they're getting ready to give you favor, blessings, and reward. For the Bible says in Isaiah 43:19, "Behold, I will do a new thing;

now it shall spring forth; shall ye not know it? I will even make a way in the wilderness, and rivers in the desert." Mephibosheth thought David was going to give him judgement and wrath, but God gave him:

1. **A new place**
2. **A new provision**
3. **A new parent**

From these examples, God is saying that He's getting ready to locate you. He is going is take you from where you are to where He desires you to be. Mephibosheth is moved from poverty to prosperity, misery to ministry; from a parched place to a palatial palace; from an outhouse to the white. For God says, "Your next move is going to change whole life."

We are told four times in the scripture that Mephibosheth is going to eat from the king's table. It is repeated that, "Mephibosheth, shall eat continually at the

Relentless Favor

king's table." Do me favor and say these words, *Upgrade... Boss Up ... Level Up.* God says, "NO MORE SCRAPS!" God says for you to get ready for new provisions—that the money you've been earning is too low. What I am getting ready to do for you... I'm getting ready to give you houses you didn't build and vineyards you didn't plant. I'm getting ready to turn your world all around.

Of all the things that God was doing for Mephibosheth, the most precious was the change of his relationship with King David. Mephibosheth was the enemy but now he had become family. Mephibosheth was the son of Johnathan, grandson of Saul. David was not in the genealogy of

Saul, but God wanted David to adopt Mephibosheth. God is changing the dynamics of certain relationships. Some have started wicked, but they will end up worth it. Some started sketchy, but they will end up successful. Some started rough, but eventually, they will get real. They started in pain, but purpose is coming forth. God says, "He is changing relationships."

Your name is in the mouth of your future underwriter. Your name is in the mouth of your future contributor. Your name is in the mouth of your future spouse! God is saying, He is getting ready to take you to a new place! God is changing

Relentless Favor

everything in your life because his favor is getting ready to locate you. The story of Mephibosheth is a prophetic representation of everyone that has your last name. Favor just found you! And when favor finds you, it furthers you!

When Mephibosheth gets into David's presence he falls to the ground in humility. Although his geographical location has changed; his identity is still the same. Mephibosheth considers himself a dead dog, although he has left his old location, his identity has not caught up with his new level. David tells Mephibosheth get up, and he puts a new robe on him and a new ring. Then David tells his servant to take over Mephibosheth's duties, and to have him eat at the king's table. We see from this example that Mephibosheth disability now becomes his availability.

You've been asking God, "When are You going to take this away from me?" God says He's not going to take it away from you because His grace is sufficient. His presence is made perfect in your weakness. Your disability, your weakness is now being made your availability so that God can get the glory. David tells his servants that Mephibosheth is going to eat at the king's table continually. My question for you today is: What is the life span of your favor?

Relentless Favor

Is it every three years, every seven years? Your favor's life span is forever... continuously. Mephibosheth is lame in both of his feet, but when you sit at the king's table, he covers what's disabled, he covers your weakness, he covers your tender parts.

Despite Mephibosheth coming from a disgraced, doomed, and destitute family; God found him. I don't know who your mother is, or who your father is. Yes, you came through your mother and from your father; however, the Bible says in Ephesians 1:4, "He hath chosen us in him before the foundation of the world."
So, when God said in Genesis 1:3, "let there be light", you were right there with Him because we are from Him. Despite your familiar background, favor is finding you!

Dr. Travis C. Jennings

Chapter 6:

Relentless FAVOR

Now Joseph had been taken down to Egypt; and Potiphar, an Egyptian officer of Pharaoh, the captain of the [royal] guard, bought him from the Ishmaelites, who had taken him down there. The LORD was with Joseph, and he [even though a slave] became a successful and prosperous man; and he was in the house of his master, the Egyptian. Now his master saw that the LORD was with him and that the LORD caused all that he did to prosper (succeed) in his hand. So Joseph pleased Potiphar and found favor in his sight and he served him as his personal servant. He made Joseph overseer over his house, and he put all that he owned in Joseph's charge.

(Genesis 39:1-4)

So, Joseph's master took him and put him in the prison, a place where the king's prisoners were confined; so, he was there in the prison. But the LORD was with Joseph and extended lovingkindness to him and gave him favor in the sight of the warden. The warden committed to Joseph's care (management) all the prisoners who were in the prison; so that whatever was done there, he was [a]in charge of it. The warden paid no attention to anything that was in Joseph's care because the LORD was with him; whatever Joseph did, the LORD made to prosper.

(Genesis 39:20-23)

You see a common thread throughout the text above. Joseph was in the pit and God was with him. Then he goes to Potiphar, from the pit, as a slave and God was with him. Then he was in prison, and God was with him. In all these cases there was one thing in common and that was favor.

Dr. Travis C. Jennings

The Favor of God is relentless, and it doesn't let you go. The Bible says that even in prison; the goodness, the mercy, the Lord's kindness showed up. The favor that is upon your life will endure the famine, the failure, and even the fracture you just came out of. I want you to know that the divorce did not destroy the favor, nor did the sickness destroy the favor. I want you to know when they laid you off and furlough you, that did not destroy the Favor of God upon your life. Your children might be going crazy, your body might be in pain. Regardless of your children, regardless of your health, none of that destroys favor. The Favor of God is relentless.

Relentless Favor

Relentless people are those people who don't accept failure. A classic type, **A personality**—they tend to be very competitive and have a strong sense of accomplishment. They are poor when it comes to impulse control. They are always active and feel like they always need to be doing something. Relentless people are like bulldogs. When they put their teeth into something, get their grip into something, or put their faith/might into something, this person with that personality will not give up. When the Favor of God is upon you, it will not turn you loose. When the Favor of God is upon you it will not let you go – It is Relentless!

Dr. Travis C. Jennings

The Favor of God is like a bulldog. Many people believe that the Favor of God happens when the atmosphere is fair. I've come to let you know that the Favor of God is beyond your "fair" atmosphere. The Favor of God is a command – it is a deposition that God places on his people. It says in the Bible in Psalm 102:13, "That it is the time to favor her, yes the set time has come." Can I tell you something? When you have the Favor of God you can go through sickness and come out successful. When you have the Favor of God you can go through pain and come out with power. When you have the Favor of God you can go through disaster and come out developed. When you have the Favor of God upon you, it will sink its teeth into you.

Now, this favor goes the distance despite problems, perplexities, and persecution. When the dust settles, your favor will be still be standing. Relentless Favor goes the distance. Relentless favor means you may be fighting doubt and unbelief, but you know if God said it than you believe it. Again, did you not know that God is not a man that He should lie, neither is He the son of man that He should repent? If He said it, He'll do it; if He spoke it, He shall bring it to pass. In understanding relentless Favor, you must first have these (3) C's:

Consciousness – you must have 24 hours a day, seven days a week consciousness about the Favor of God. When you get up in the morning you know that this is the day that the Lord has made, and you will be glad and rejoice in it. You understand that favor surrounds you like a shield. When you have a consciousness about the Favor of God, you will never let certain things come out your mouth that is the opposite of your purpose, against your potential, or against your process.

Consistency – believers must speak life and have a winner's attitude regardless of what's going. Regardless of the trial, regardless of the test, you must have an attitude that, "I'm going to speak the word of God regardless of the winds and the fiery furnaces. I'm going to speak the word of God, because the word of God is a lamp unto my feet and a light unto my path. I might be in the fiery furnace, but I know God is with me. I will come out and God will get serious glory!"

Commitment – you must be willing to commit to the previous two. You must understand that whatever you say in faith, the process is opposite of the word of God. You must be careful not to allow the test to stop your faith. You can't allow the trial to forfeit your promise, because the promises of God are yea and amen. The sweat is producing enough stamina for the supernatural to show up. I want to talk to someone that have been working on something; you've been grinding, and you haven't been public on social media. God told me to tell you, "Work in silence and let your success be your noise." God is getting ready to give you a certain reveal date, and every eye will know that God is in your life.

This chapter is to expose the flawed thinking that favor is without a fight. Listen, favor comes because of the fight. I would like to reveal the fascinating truth that favor is produced because of the fight, and it is because of that fight that you have favor. It's an interesting truth that favor not only brings increase, but it brings a new identity. It happened to Jacob when he was fighting against the angel, and he won (Genesis 32). The Bible lets us know that because Jacob fought with the angel, God granted him a new identity. Look at Moses. His favor came because he stood against Pharaoh (Exodus 7). Shadrach, Meshach, and Abednego's favor came because they endured the fiery furnace (Daniel 3). Look at Esther. Her favor came because she had to go through the process of becoming queen (Esther 2). Look at Jehoshaphat. His favor came because he stood against the challenge of the enemy (1 Kings 22).

Dr. Travis C. Jennings

I've come to tell you that the trials you're going through is producing favor! That's why you can't give up. You have been through hell and highwater; you have been through warfare and weariness; and God is about to bring you out to the winner's circle. Paul said it best in 1 Timothy 6:12, "Fight the good faith of fight and lay ahold to eternal life." I've come to tell you that favor is not free. That's why you cannot give up on God! You cannot return to your vomit or go back to your perversion! Remember, favor is not free!

Many people come to church, and they give God a, "Yes, Lord;" but their 'Yes, Lord' is empty. I want to talk to somebody

Relentless Favor

whose, "Yes, Lord," cost them everything. A 'Yes, Lord" is very expensive. The favor on your life is not free. You've had to sacrifice for this favor. You've had to pray and fast for this favor. You've had to lay between the porch and the altar for this favor. The Bible says is best in Psalm 34:19, "Many are the afflictions of the righteous, but the LORD delivers him from them all."

That's why you didn't give up or turn away. That is why you didn't back slide. That is why you couldn't turn your back on your calling. The reason you could not destroy your destiny is because of the fight. The reason you could not cancel your assignment or destroy your destiny is because you fought for it! Give God praise for the fight!

I'm reminded of my testimony: the birth, the brokenness, the burden, the belief, the beauty, and even the best. The Bible tells us in Revelation 12:11, that they overcame "by the blood of the Lamb and by the word of their testimony." When I look back over my life, my mother was 14 years old, and my father was 21 years. They came together and produced a prophet. My upbringing was very unconventional. It was not according to the standard of many. God put these two people together and produced a little boy. From the time I was born I was full of rejection, abandonment, rebellion, and pride. My mother gave me up and so as a result I was raised by my great grandmother. You see, because of my brokenness and rejection I was depressed, suicidal, and full of hatred. I never felt the love of my mother or father and that prevented me from being validated as a child. When a child is not validated by their parents, they don't have any direction, nor do they know their full potential.

The burden that I was faced with as a child caused me to sink into the quicksand of generational curses. I went through life like a candle in the wind. I was living my life full of hatred and destruction. I didn't care about dying, even planned my own suicide. One Saturday morning, I found a bottle of sleeping pills and I took the entire bottle. The devil had convinced me that I was my father's and mother's curse. Then, God did something in my life at the age of 14 and shifted me into a belief.

I went to a sanctified church and heard the gospel of Jesus Christ preached to me. It was during that church service that God set me free! I started reading the Word of God and living my life the way God said. I read in the scripture that I was to lend and not borrow – I believed it. I read that I am fearfully and wonderfully made – I believed it. I read that I am a royal priesthood, and I am a holy nation – I believed it. Then David said in Psalms, "When my mother and my father forsake me, the Lord will take me up."

I started seeing myself through the eyes of the blood. I found in the Word of God in 2 Corinthians 5:17, "If any man be in Christ, he is a new creature, old things are passed away, behold all things become new." I started to see myself like the righteousness of God in Jesus. I started seeing myself how God sees me. I found out that regardless of whether or not my father was in my life, or my parents cared for me, God told me that I would be a successful husband and father. Even though I had never seen it before, His Word gave me the assurance that I could do all things through Him! I found out that I had the ability to love and change lives.

Then, I met a girl by the name of Stephanie LaShaun, and I fell in love for the first time. Stephanie and I got married and we had to sleep on the floor and eat peanut butter sandwiches. But God said, "Travis, I'm going to teach you faith, and faith comes by hearing My Word." So, Stephanie and I got up every morning, and we decreed and declared that "Wealth and riches was in our house." God took a little boy and little girl and placed His favor on us. I was the bastard of my family, and now, I am the wealthiest. I was the most broken of my

Relentless Favor

family, and now I'm the priest who mends hearts through my brothers and my mother. God knows how to flip the script in our lives. That is what God has done for me!

I've come to let you know what relentless Favor did for Travis. It followed me through the birth, the brokenness, the burden, the belief, the beauty, and caused me to live my best life! My testimony is to God be the glory for the great things he has done! God told me that the relentless favor that is on my life is also on your life! Regardless of the trials you're going through, favor is on you. Regardless of the trouble you're in, favor is on you.

Dr. Travis C. Jennings

Relentless, Favor is showing up in every area of your life!

About the Author:

The ultimate INFLUENCER, Dr. Travis Jennings, a trailblazer, and 21st-century reformer, is an author, entrepreneur, executive producer, philanthropist, life-coach, husband, and father. Dr. Jennings has personally sold thousands of books globally. He's guided the careers and the launching of other new authors and new entrepreneurs, helping to advance the kingdom. He is the Senior Pastor of the Harvest Tabernacle in Atlanta.

Dr. Travis C. Jennings

He embodies relentless favor and this manuscript will cause you to walk boldly into favor of God upon your life.